AF580351

That's Me — TYLER!

By Frances Burton

Illustrated by Karmen Thompson

With thanks to Marge Grutzmacher
("Mrs. G")

THAT'S ME — TYLER

Written by Frances Burton

Illustrated by Karmen Thompson

Stonehill Publishing
P.O. Box 250
Ephraim, WI 54211

ISBN 0-9650769-2-X

Designed by Jane Tenenbaum

Printed in Singapore

This true story is dedicated
to the memory of
Champion Loteki That's My Style
(Tyler) who traveled the world
with Grammy Award© winning
pianist John Browning.

That's me — Tyler!
I'm a Papillon.
"Papillon" means butterfly in French. Look at my big ears with long hair hanging down. Do you think they look like butterflies?

Well, I'm not a butterfly.

I'm a dog.

I'm just very small,
about the size of a kitten.

When I was only a puppy
I knew I was special.
I heard people say,
"Tyler will be a champion some day."

When I grew up I won lots of prizes
and I did become a champion!
But I knew I was even more special than that.

What would I do next?

Then a man named John came to visit. He said he was searching for a special dog.

That's me — Tyler!

John needed a friend,
so I gave him a kiss and
snuggled into his arms.
He looked down at me
and smiled. He had
found his special dog.

I soon discovered John didn't know much about dogs. I would have to teach him.

He closed me in the bathroom because he thought I would piddle on his rugs. I thumped my tail against the door as hard as I could and howled.

I just wanted to be with John.

He opened the door and
I walked out. Now we
understood each other.

I am his friend and
he is mine.

John and I go everywhere together. He never leaves me at home. I get into my traveling bag and John puts it over his shoulder.

It's soft and cozy in there with little holes in the sides so I can breathe and see outside. John is happy that I go with him.

At the grocery store I see people pushing their carts. I smell vegetables and meat and cookies. I hear people talking.

I’m very quiet but sometimes shoppers see me peeking out and say, “Look at the cute little dog.“

That’s me — Tyler!

John likes to eat in restaurants.
I stay in my bag under his chair.
Oh, it smells so-o-o-o good in a restaurant.

Sometimes I wiggle the zipper on my bag. I poke my nose out and sniff. Then I squirm out and visit nearby tables.

People are surprised to see me. I usually collect a few tidbits before John discovers what I've done and tucks me back in.

John is a famous pianist.

I stay near the piano and listen to him practice. I don't make any noise. He practices a lot and sometimes I fall asleep listening.

But when he finishes, I always wake up. I wag my tail back and forth as fast as I can and he says, "I'm glad you're here, Tyler."

John plays concerts far away. I go on the airplane with him.

I curl up in my bag and John puts it under his seat. It's dark in there and I hear the plane making strange noises, but as long as I'm with John I feel safe.

When I smell food my nose quivers. John is eating dinner and soon he will slip little pieces of his meal into my bag. I eat some interesting things on airplanes.

When we travel, we stay in a hotel. At night I sleep in my own kennel next to the bed. I can see John and he can see me.

But when we take a little nap before the concert, I sleep on John's bed. I settle in on one pillow and John snoozes on the other.

We ride in a taxi
to the concert hall.

While John is on stage playing, I wait backstage. I'm quiet and never bark.

Once I got to go on stage with John. I really liked that. People in the audience clapped and clapped. They said, "There's Tyler." That's me!

John meets important people and he introduces me to them.

I met the Queen of Belgium and John let her hold me. She was a nice lady but she didn't wear a crown. She looked like a grandmother.

One time the Pope blessed me.

Another time an orchestra conductor had a party for me. He served my favorite food — smoked salmon. I always behave well because I don't want to embarrass John. I know he's proud of me.

John and I have fun traveling together. We've been all over the world. It's exciting to go on trips and meet new people and sniff new smells.

Most dogs have to stay home. I know I'm lucky.

But what I like best is being John's friend.

That's a job for a very special dog.

And that's me — Tyler!